Dinosaur

JOKES

By **U.R. Phunny**

BIG BUDDY

JOKES

Big Buddy Books

An imprint of Abdo Publishing
abdopublishing.com

abdopublishing.com

Published by Abdo Publishing, a division of ABDO, PO Box 398166, Minneapolis, Minnesota 55439.
Copyright © 2017 by Abdo Consulting Group, Inc. International copyrights reserved in all countries.
No part of this book may be reproduced in any form without written permission from the publisher.
Big Buddy Books™ is a trademark and logo of Abdo Publishing.

Printed in the United States of America, North Mankato, Minnesota.
082016
012017

THIS BOOK CONTAINS
RECYCLED MATERIALS

Illustrations: Sunny Grey/Spectrum Studio

Coordinating Series Editor: Tamara L. Britton
Contributing Editor: Katie Lajiness
Graphic Design: Taylor Higgins

Publisher's Cataloging-in-Publication Data

Names: Phunny, U. R., author.
Title: Dinosaur jokes / by U. R. Phunny.
Description: Minneapolis, MN : Abdo Publishing, 2017. | Series: Big buddy jokes
Identifiers: LCCN 2016944864 | ISBN 9781680785111 (lib. bdg.) | ISBN
      9781680798715 (ebook)
Subjects: LCSH: Dinosaurs--Juvenile humor. | Wit and humor--Juvenile humor.
Classification: DDC 818/.602--dc23
LC record available at http://lccn.loc.gov/2016944864

What should you do if you find a dinosaur in your bed?

Find somewhere else to sleep!

Did you hear the joke about the dinosaur egg?

It cracked me up!

What has a spiked tail, plates on its back, and 16 wheels?

A stegosaurus on roller skates!

What do you call a *Tyrannosaurus rex* when it wears a cowboy hat and boots?

Tyrannosaurus Tex!

What do you call a worried dinosaur?

A nervous wrecks!

What do you call a dinosaur that never gives up?

A try-try-try-ceratops!

What do you get when you cross a dinosaur with fireworks?

Dino-mite!

What do you get when you give a dinosaur a pogo stick to play with?

Big holes in your driveway!

What do you call a triceratops that talks and talks and talks?

A dino-bore!

7

What is as big as a dinosaur but weighs nothing?

Its shadow!

What do dinosaurs use to decorate their bathrooms?

Rep-tiles!

What do you do when a dinosaur sneezes?

You get out of the way!

Why doesn't the *T. rex* skeleton attack the museum visitors?

Because she has no guts!

What do you get if you cross a dinosaur with a pig?

Jurassic Pork!

Where did the velociraptor buy things?

At a dino-store!

What do you call a dinosaur that was elected to Congress?

Rep. Tile!

How can you tell if a dinosaur is a vegetarian?

Lie down on a plate.

Did you hear about the invisible dinosaur that went to the hospital?

The doctor couldn't see her!

Why did the dinosaur get a ticket?

He was in a no stomping zone.

What do you get if you cross a dinosaur with a wizard?

A Tyrannosaurus hex!

What came after the dinosaur?

Its tail!

What was the most flexible dinosaur?

Tyrannosaurus flex!

Why did the apatosaurus devour the factory?

Because she was a plant eater!

What did the dinosaur call her shirt-making business?

Try Sara's Tops.

Which type of dinosaur could jump higher than a house?

Any kind! A house can't jump!

What dinosaur was a photographer?

A camera-saurus!

What kind of dinosaur cried a lot?

Tear-annosaurus.

How do dinosaurs pay their bills?

With Tyrannosaurus checks!

What do you call a brontosaurus that drives a racing car?

A pronto bronto!

What did the dinosaur say when he saw the volcano erupt?

What a lava-ly day!

What do you call 100 dancing dinosaurs?

An earthquake!

What do you call a fossil that doesn't want to work?

Lazy bones!

How do baby pteranodons learn to fly?

They wing it!

Its tricera-bottom!

20

Why do dinosaurs eat raw meat?

Because they don't know how to cook!

What was wrong with the dinosaur's car?

A flat tire-annosaurus!

What vehicle does *T. rex* use to go from planet to planet?

A dino-saucer!

What do you get when you cross a *T. rex* and a chicken?

Tyrannosaurus pecks!

Where do prehistoric reptiles like to go on vacation?

To the dino-shore!

What do you get if you cross a triceratops with a kangaroo?

A tricera-hops!

Why shouldn't you tell secrets to dinosaurs?

Because they have big mouths!

Why did the dinosaur put on a bandage?

He had a dino-sore!

How do you ask a dinosaur to lunch?

Tea, Rex?

Why did the archaeopteryx catch the worm?

Because it was an early bird!

What do you call a plated dinosaur when he sleeps?

A stego-snorus!

What dinosaur would you find in a rodeo?

A bronco-saurus!

What was the scariest prehistoric animal?

The terror-dactyl!

What's the best way to talk to a dinosaur?

Long distance!

Why are all the dinosaur bones in the museum old?

Cause they can't afford new ones!

Which dinosaur is the smartest?

Thesaurus!

What dinosaur loves pancakes?

Tri-syrup-tops!

What do you call a dinosaur that eats automobiles?

A car-nivore!

Why do stegosauruses get invited to dinner?

Because they bring their own plates!

What do you say when you meet a two-headed dinosaur?

Hi! Hi!

What makes more noise than a dinosaur?

Two dinosaurs!

Why did the dinosaur cross the road?

It was the chicken's day off.

What's better than a talking dinosaur?

B-E-E!

A spelling bee!

WEBSITES

To learn more about Big Buddy Jokes, visit **booklinks.abdopublishing.com**. These links are routinely monitored and updated to provide the most current information available.